Succulents
Made Easy

A Beginner's Guide

TOKIIRO

TUTTLE Publishing

Tokyo | Rutland, Vermont | Singapore

CONTENTS

PART 5
Asteraceae

PART 6
Crassulaceae

How to Use This Book

This book is divided into five sections to cover rosette-form Crassulaceae, Liliaceae, Cactaceae, Asteraceae and other Crassulaceae.

Each chapter is divided into two sections: the pages that show the steps to creating an arrangement which features mainly plants from that particular family, and illustrated reference pages to show the plants that are typical in that family. As you read, you will learn the techniques for creating a group planting and at the same time acquire knowledge about succulents.

Arrangement (group planting) pages

Creating a gorgeous bouquet-like arrangement

When putting together the arrangement, start by visualizing the world expressed in the container. Here, we're making a bouquet-like arrangement that spills out over the sides. Large, rosette types with a sense of presence, such as Echeveria derenbergii and Graptoveria titubans play the leading roles, with makinoi 'Aurea' and lineare f.variegata from the Sedum family used as ground cover. It's a lineup that allows the gradations of green to be shown to their advantage.

When creating an arrangement, it is important to use dry soil. If it is moist, it won't give plants the vitality needed to put out new roots.

Example combination for a rosette-form Crassulaceae arrangement

1. Sedum makinoi 'Aurea'
2. Sedum spurium 'Dragon's Blood'
3. Echeveria derenbergii
4. Echeveria 'Peach Pride'
5. Crassula lycopodioides var pseudolycopodioides
6. Sedum makinoi
7. Crassula sarmentosa
8. Sedum lineare f.variegata
9. Echeveria 'Yourou'
10. Graptoveria titubans

Pour in soil to cover stones

PART 2

1 If at all possible, select a container with a hole in the base. The hole allows for better drainage.

2

3 Cut mesh and place it in the pot base to cover the hole.

4

5 Place stones into the container so that about the size of a cup is left free. Using a lot of stones improves drainage.

6

7 Pour in soil to cover stones. If too much soil is added, it won't be possible to plant the succulents, so keep this in mind.

18

19

Title and explanatory notes

This covers the theme of the arrangement, points to keep in mind when creating it, tips for creating a good result and so on. Deepening your understanding will improve your ability to create attractive arrangements, so make sure to read this and take it in.

Examples of combinations for arrangements

Here, we introduce examples of combinations of plants used in the arrangement. Being able to see the names and numbers at a glance allows you to check them against the illustrated reference and get an understanding of their characteristics and so on.

Steps for creating the arrangement

The steps for creating the arrangement are explained for easy comprehension via photos and text. Looking at the photos while working on the arrangement will improve the end result. Furthermore, some pages feature a section called "Close up" which offers advice on slightly more advanced techniques and how to work smoothly.

Prior to starting on any of the group plantings in this book, it's a good idea to read through the instructions before even assembling your plants, tools and materials.

At the end of each chapter, we have included tips on cultivation. Getting a grasp of these will allow you to grow healthy, attractively-shaped succulents.

You may like to read right from the start, or prefer to look only at the pages that interest you. Please use the book in the way that suits you best.

Illustrated reference charts

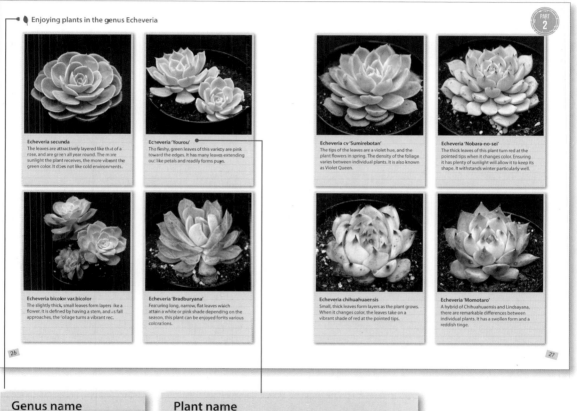

Genus name
The genus (group) name for the plants mentioned is listed here, so it can be seen at a glance.

Plant name
The photo and name of the plant are listed here, along with an explanation of its characteristics. Refer to this when creating arrangements and when caring for plants. It is also useful information when choosing plants. In addition, plants are listed in a table of contents on the pages before the illustrated references in each chapter, so use this when you want to search for a name.

Why We Wrote This Book

Succulents are plants that mainly grow natively in arid desert regions such as southern Africa and Mexico. They are characterized by their plump, sumptuous leaves and stems which store water in order to withstand the harsh environment.

More and more people are discovering the charm of their adorable thick, rounded forms, and while they are naturally sold at gardening stores, they are also popular at stores selling general merchandise. The fact that they do not require daily watering and are relatively easy to cultivate may also explain their popularity.

In this book, we'll cover succulents that are fairly easy to come by and suggest ways to display them that combine plants of the same species. This book will be useful in a variety of situations for learning about, cultivating and arranging succulents, such as discovering succulents you like by looking at shapes, properties and characteristics of the varieties listed, or to research details of a succulent you've found in a store.

We hope this book will help you understand the characteristics of succulents and how to cultivate them in order to add healing and color to your daily life.

—**TOKIIRO**

PART 1
The Appeal of Succulents

Cultivate lively succulents by placing them in arrangements they'll love

Simply displaying a succulent by a gate or just out the front of a dwelling creates a cheerful impression. There are various colors and shapes depending on the type, but putting a plant in light, gentle hues out on display is sure to soothe a body and mind tired from the busyness of daily life.

The fun of arranging succulents

Succulents are lovely even when the same types are planted together in a pot, but a group planting arrangement creates a display that brightens and enlivens the space even more. The beauty of their appearance; the joy felt in raising healthy, vital plants; and the pleasure gained from the evolving form of the arrangement as the plants grow and seasons change—all of these contribute to the appeal of succulents.

Understanding their origins is extremely helpful

Plants use carbon dioxide, water and sunlight to perform photosynthesis. The pigment chlorophyll produces glucose, a nutrient that is essential to plants' growth, and when cultivating plants, it is important to maintain a balance of light and water to facilitate photosynthesis.

For this reason, it is important to have a knowledge of the origins of the plants you are growing. Succulents' light and water requirements vary depending on their natural habitat and their various qualities. As they are very often being cultivated in a climate different from that of their natural habitat, make every effort to create an environment similar to that of their place of origin. In theory, they grow best outdoors where there is bright sunlight and good ventilation. Rather than deciding to water a certain number of times per month, check the plants' condition and water accordingly.

Consider the environment and season when positioning succulents

A bright, sunny spot with good ventilation is ideal for succulents, but during long periods of wet weather such as the rainy season it's necessary to shift them to somewhere they can avoid the rain. If the leaves get wet, the "stomata" which absorb carbon dioxide will close. On succulents, the stomata open up at night, so take particular care during long periods of rain at night.

Furthermore, winters in cold regions and high temperatures at the peak of summer create harsh conditions for succulents, so exercise judgment at those times and move them indoors or into the shade. However, make sure when moving them that they do not experience sudden changes in temperature.

Water in a timely manner, taking the environment into account

Depending on where they are being cultivated, the amount of available sunlight will vary, and there are also differences due to the plant species, season and so on. These factors need to be taken into account when determining the frequency of watering. It's best only to water when the plant requires it, so it's important to always be on the lookout for changes in its condition.

Additionally, when watering, give enough water so that it runs out from the hole in the base of the pot. Not moistening the leaves, but rather directing the water at the soil is key.

Assembling the tools needed

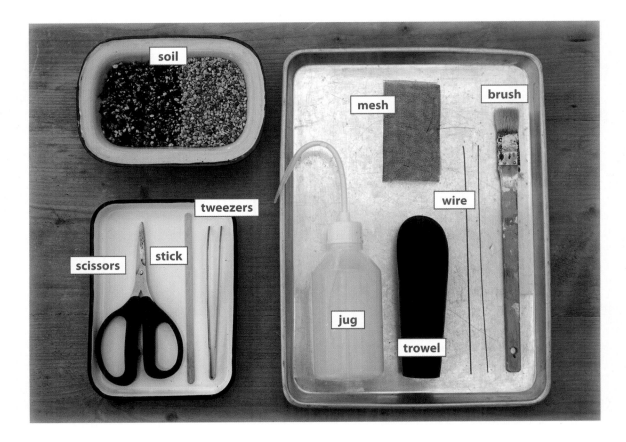

When you're ready to start on an arrangement, make sure you have all the basic tools and materials to hand. Choose tools and equipment with delicate tasks in mind, making sure to select fine mesh, for example. Coffee stirrers or disposable chopsticks can be used as sticks. In terms of soil, use the type specifically for succulents that can be found at gardening stores. The roots will take well if relatively fine soil is selected for an arrangement. If planting just one type by itself, it's fine to use coarser soil.

Blend the soil to suit the arrangement
Mixing culture soil for flowers into the soil aids water retention, so this is an effective measure for plants that like water. Once you get more particular, you can try blending several different soil types.

PART 2
Rosette Crassulaceae

Creating group plantings to highlight the flower-like leaf formations

Hints for rosette-form Crassulaceae plantings

The Crassulaceae family is one of the most popular of all the succulents. Many of them originate in arid regions and there are many varieties. Growing out in a radial or spiral formation, the leaves are said to form a "rosette" or "rosetta," and the flower-like form is extremely appealing. Here, we focus on the genus Echeveria—which is particularly well known for its rosette-like shape—to create an attractive arrangement.

Creating a gorgeous bouquet-like arrangement

When putting together the arrangement, start by visualizing the world expressed in the container. Here, we're making a bouquet-like arrangement that spills out over the sides. Large, rosette types with a sense of presence, such as Echeveria derenbergii and Graptoveria titubans play the leading roles, with makinoi 'Aurea' and lineare f.variegata from the Sedum family used as ground cover. It's a lineup that allows the gradations of green to be shown to their advantage.

When creating an arrangement, it is important to use dry soil. If it is moist, it won't give plants the vitality needed to put out new roots.

Example combination for a rosette-form Crassulaceae arrangement

1　Sedum makinoi 'Aurea'
2　Sedum spurium 'Dragon's Blood'
3　Echeveria derenbergii
4　Echeveria 'Peach Pride'
5　Crassula lycopodioides var pseudolycopodioides
6　Sedum makinoi
7　Crassula sarmentosa
8　Sedum lineare f.variegata
9　Echeveria 'Yourou'
10　Graptoveria titubans

Pour in soil to cover stones

1

If at all possible, select a container with a hole in the base. The hole allows for better drainage.

2

3

Cut mesh and place it in the pot base to cover the hole.

4

5

Place stones into the container so that about the size of a cup is left free. Using a lot of stones improves drainage.

6

7

Pour in soil to cover stones. If too much soil is added, it won't be possible to place the succulents, so keep this in mind.

8

9

Remove each plant from its pot by holding the pot in both hands and pressing around the sides.

10

Hold the leaf section and gently draw the plant upwards. If you pull it out while the plant is facing down, soil will go all over the leaves.

11

Use your fingers to massage the roots and lightly remove soil. This allows the roots to take well when planted. It also naturally removes any damaged roots along with the soil.

CLOSE UP

Divide stock that has a lot of roots

For plants such as sedum varieties, which have a lot of roots, it is difficult to loosen the roots, so rather than brushing off the soil, divide them by hand to incorporate into the arrangement. Removing them from their pot is the same—press the sides with your fingers and draw the plant upwards.

12

Remove other plants from their pots in the same way and loosen the roots.

13

Plant Graptoveria titubans at the edge of the container. Hold the plant in place with your hand as you tip the soil in to secure it.

Tips for arranging and combining rosette-form Crassulaceae

✓ As the rosette types look circular when viewed from overhead, spaces are left between them when planted. It's a good idea to fill the gaps in with ground cover plants.
✓ Don't secure them too firmly when planting.

14

Plant Sedum lineare f.variegata next to Graptoveria titubans. This sort of plant which is used to fill gaps is called "ground cover" and is divided into small pieces for planting.

15

In the same way, plant Sedum makinoi 'Aurea' as ground cover. It's a good idea to use tweezers when planting into small spaces.

16

Plant Crassula sarmentosa in the center. For delicate plants, use tweezers when positioning them into the soil.

Plant the finely divided Crassula lycopodioides var. pseudolycopodioides next to the Crassula sarmentosa.

Add soil where needed to suit the arrangement.

Plant Sedum makinoi to appear as if it is spilling out from the container.

Tips for arranging and combining rosette-form Crassulaceae

✓ The look of the arrangement will change depending on how the ground cover colors combine with the other plants.
✓ Position a plant with height in the center to achieve a roughly circular result.

Once a few succulents are planted, entwine neighboring plants around each other. This evokes the look of plants that have grown naturally, so doing this lends the arrangement solidity and the appearance that it has been growing for some time.

Before planting, sandwich pieces of Sedum makinoi 'Aurea' into Echeveria 'Yourou'. Sandwiching plants together from the start makes for a more natural-looking arrangement.

23 Plant the combined Echeveria 'Yourou' and Sedum makinoi 'Aurea' into the edge of the pot.

24 Plant Sedum spurium 'Dragon's Blood' into the center and entwine it with other succulents such as Crassula sarmentosa. Gather tall plants in the center to create height.

25 Plant Echeveria 'Peach Pride' next to Echeveria 'Yourou'.

26 Plant Echeveria derenbergii into the remaining space and fill in any gaps with ground cover.

27

28 Use the stick to press in the soil and the brush to dust soil off the side of the container. Wind plants around each other to finish off the arrangement.

Illustrated references for Echeveria (Crassulaceae)

There are more than 180 species in the Echeveria genus, which is the main rosette type in the Crassulaceae family. There is a huge range of sizes and colors, so it is a good idea to bring various types together in a group planting. The lack of a stem is one of their defining features. Watch out for pest infestations, which may occur occasionally.

25

🍃 Enjoying plants in the genus Echeveria

Echeveria secunda
The leaves are attractively layered like that of a rose, and are green all year round. The more sunlight the plant receives, the more vibrant the green color. It does not like cold environments.

Echeveria 'Yourou'
The fleshy, green leaves of this variety are pink toward the edges. It has many leaves extending out like petals and readily forms pups.

Echeveria bicolor var.bicolor
The slightly thick, small leaves form layers like a flower. It is defined by having a stem, and as fall approaches, the foliage turns a vibrant red.

Echeveria 'Bradburyana'
Featuring long, narrow, flat leaves which attain a white or pink shade depending on the season, this plant can be enjoyed for its various colorations.

Echeveria cv 'Sumirebotan'

The tips of the leaves are a violet hue, and the plant flowers in spring. The density of the foliage varies between individual plants. It is also known as Violet Queen.

Echeveria 'Nobara-no-sei'

The thick leaves of this plant turn red at the pointed tips when it changes color. Ensuring it has plenty of sunlight will allow it to keep its shape. It withstands winter particularly well.

Echeveria chihuahuaensis

Small, thick leaves form layers as the plant grows. When it changes color, the leaves take on a vibrant shade of red at the pointed tips.

Echeveria 'Momotaro'

A hybrid of Chihuahuaensis and Lindsayana, there are remarkable differences between individual plants. It has a swollen form and a reddish tinge.

Enjoying plants in the genus Echeveria

Graptoveria titubans
The thick leaves grow in the same way as a rose flower and are a white-tinged green with pink tips. The plant grows from spring through to summer and is dormant in winter.

Echeveria runyonii
The white-tinged leaves are outlined in a vibrant shade of pink, and the plant changes little in appearance regardless of the season. It is covered in a white powder that thickens the more sun it gets.

Echeveria 'Splendor'
The small, fleshy, folded leaves of this variety form rows, with the plant putting out its distinctively shaped flowers in fall. It is also called Top Splendor.

Echeveria 'Crystal'
This plant has long, slender, rounded leaves in a pale shade of green with pointed ends that turn red when the leaves change color. It likes sunlight and appears to be dusted with a white powder.

Graptoveria 'Caerulescens'

Resilient against cold, this plant can tolerate temperatures down to 28–30° F (- 1–2° C). The body becomes more compact in winter to withstand the cold. Yellow flowers bloom from the side of the plant in spring.

Echeveria 'Afterglow'

This variety has attractive leaves in a purple hue dusted with white. The color forms as if to frame the leaves, and can be enjoyed all year round.

Echeveria derenbergii

The small, faintly colored leaves of this variety form several layers. The ends of the leaves turn red when the plant changes color and it has orange flowers in spring.

Echeveria 'Lola'

The white-tinged pale coloring of the fleshy leaves defines this plant. The red-tipped leaves grow inward at the center. It is temperature-sensitive, so take care in the summer.

🍃 Enjoying plants in the genus Encheveria

Echeveria 'lilacina'
The slightly flat leaves are rounded in shape and dusted with white. They grow in layers, extending outwards and turning a pale pink when the plant changes color.

Echeveria peacockii
The slender, long, white leaves form layers as they grow and are covered with a white powder. The plant has yellow flowers in summer and copes well with dry conditions. It is the strain from which varieties such as Echeveria 'Yourou' originate.

Echeveria peacockii Princess Pearl
An attractive variety with white powder dusting its leaves. Insufficient sunlight reduces the covering of powder, so care is needed.

Echeveria 'Bombycina'
A hybrid variety of Echeveria setosa and Echeveria pulvinata. The small, rounded leaves are covered all over with hairs. It forms a stem as it grows.

Echeveria harmsii
The small, slender, long leaves are covered all over with hair. The plant grows vertically and turns red around the leaves, as if forming an outline, when the plant changes color.

Echeveria pulvinata
Long, narrow and fleshy, the leaves of this variety are covered with hairs. Usually green, the tips turn red when the plant changes color. The stem forms as the plant grows.

Echeveria pulvinata 'Frosty'
The small, spatula-like leaves are covered in hairs that are soft to the touch. The plant grows vertically, forming stems and branching as it grows.

Echeveria 'Powder Blue'
Usually colored with a bluish tinge, the thin leaves turn an attractive, gradually deepening pink when the plant changes color. It is relatively easy to increase stock of this plant.

🌿 Enjoying plants in the genus Echeveria

Echeveria 'Takasagono-Okina'
A unique variety with a fold-like appearance, this plant flowers in fall, with the entire plant turning an attractive shade of red.

Echeveria 'Perle von Nurnberg'
This variety has beautiful purple leaves, with reddish flowers in the spring. As it tends to attract scale insects and cotton bugs, anti-pest measures are necessary.

Echeveria 'Purposorum'
Flowering in summer, this variety is a reddish color and has an adorable bud-like shape. There are many varieties with different leaf formations available.

Echeveria 'Golden Glow'
The leaves of this variety have a subtle red tinge around the edges. In spring, reddish flowers bloom at the sides of the plant stock. Except for the winter months, anti-pest measures are necessary.

Echeveria 'Gungekka'
Characterized by the way it sprouts and grows in clusters. A fairly slow-growing plant, it becomes more compact in fall and starts to put on some color.

Echeveria shaviana
A variety with pale purple leaves, it extends boldly out as it grows. In summer, it has flowers in a purple color similar to that of the leaves.

Echeveria Subsessillis
A hybrid variety with adorable purple edges around the deep green leaves. It requires moderate sun exposure even in winter.

🍃 Enjoying plants in the genus Echeveria

Graptoveria 'Komurasaki'
The flat, pointy-tipped leaves are a reddish shade that deepens to almost black. Native to Central America, it is also known as Afinis.

Echeveria 'Mebina'
The green and pink gradation of the leaves make this an attractive variety. It sprouts in clusters and has yellow flowers in spring.

Echeveria 'Baron Bold'
A hybrid, this plant is characterized by the protrusions on its leaves. It extends vertically as it grows. In summer, It has vivid red flowers.

Echeveria pulidonis
Edged in red, the green leaves of this variety extend far out as it grows. It has yellow flowers in spring and the tips of the leaves turn red in fall.

Echeveria 'Iria'
Growing by forming clusters from side shoots, this plant has yellow flowers in spring. It copes well with heat and cold, but watch out for mold when it is humid.

Echeveria Spruce Oliver
Characterized by the red edging around its green leaves, this plant extends vertically as it grows. In spring it has red flowers, and the tips of the leaves turn red in fall.

Echeveria 'Deresseana'
This variety is defined by its green leaves tinged with white. It is similar to Echeveria 'Kokoro' in appearance, but has broader leaves.

Echeveria carnicolor
This variety has attractive leaves in a purple hue tinged with white. It gets larger and extends out as it grows. In spring it has red flowers. The entire plant changes color in fall.

Enjoying plants in the genus Echeveria

Echeveria 'Yamatobini'
A hybrid variety featuring glossy, deep green leaves. In spring, it has flowers in various colors, and the plant changes color in fall. It is robust and relatively easy to grow.

Echeveria 'Jyusou'
Characterized by leaves covered with soft hairs, this plant branches out and spreads vertically as it grows. In spring it has orange flowers.

Echeveria 'Dondo'
The fine hairs covering its green leaves and the pink coloring at the leaf tips make this an adorable variety. It has orange flowers in spring.

Pachyveria 'Powder Puff'
Featuring whitish leaves, this plant spreads outwards as it grows. It increases by division and grows at a normal rate.

Echeveria 'Van Breen'
The depth of the leaves makes an impression in this variety, which grows by extending outwards. In spring it has orange flowers.

Echeveria Princess Pearl
Characterized by large, purple creased leaves, this variety spreads outwards as it grows. It changes color in fall.

Echeveria 'Midoribotan'
This variety has fleshy leaves in a bright green color and blossoms with orange flowers in spring. It does not cope well with heat, so requires particular care in summer.

Echeveria laui
The white leaves covered with a white powder make this an attractive variety. It is robust and copes relatively well with both heat and cold, but is prone to moldering, so needs to be kept in a well-ventilated spot.

Enjoying plants in the genus Echeveria

Graptoveria 'Purple King'
As its name suggests, this variety has attractive purple leaves. In spring, it has yellow flowers. It is vulnerable to heat and moldering in the summer months, so care is needed.

Echeveria afinis
This large variety has fleshy leaves in a blackish color. In fall, it has vivid red flowers. It is relatively resilient to heat and cold.

Echeveria 'Ron Evans'
A hybrid variety with attractive green and orange coloring. It grows to a large size by spreading out. In spring it has orange flowers, and the plant changes color in fall.

Aeonium goochiae
Characterized by wide, purple leaves, this variety spreads to a large size. Its appearance is similar to that of the Perle von Nurnberg.

Pachyveria 'Scheideckeri'

Characterized by its purple leaves, this variety has yellow flowers in spring. It is vulnerable to heat and the extreme humidity of summer makes it prone to black spot disease, so make sure to keep it in a well-ventilated spot.

Echeveria 'Deren-Oliver'

Featuring bright green leaves, this variety extends vertically as it grows. In spring, it puts out orange flowers from the sides. It changes color in fall.

Echeveria 'Rezry'

Characterized by fleshy leaves tinged with red, this variety extends vertically as it grows. In fall it turns purple. It is relatively resilient to heat and cold.

Enjoying plants in the genus Echeveria

Echeveria 'Peach Pride'

A hybrid variety with attractive, green, rounded leaves. It extends vertically to grow and has red flowers in spring.

Echeveria setosa var.minor

This variety is defined by the blue hairs growing on the surfaces of its fleshy leaves, which have purple undersides. It is resilient to cold but is slightly vulnerable to heat.

Echeveria 'Spectabilis'

The fluffy hairs covering the leaves make this an adorable variety. The leaves are tipped with a purple color. It extends vertically as it grows. It significantly resembles Echeveria 'Set Oliver'.

The origins of the Echeveria genus

The Echeveria genus has its origins in Central America, Mexico, the southwest of North America and South Africa. Its name is said to be derived from the botanical artist Atanasio Echeverria, who illustrated Mexican botanical magazines during the 18th century. Plants with a diameter of up to 1" (2.5 cm) are known as "minima," while those with a diameter larger than 16" (40 cm) are called "gantea."

Illustrated references for Aeonium, Graptopetalum and Graptoveria

Classified as a rosette type in the Crassulaceae family, the Aeonium genus has its growth period in winter and has vivid, variegated leaves. The Graptopetalum genus is defined by fleshy leaves, with many varieties growing stems. The Graptoveria genus is a hybrid of the Echeveria and Graptopetalum genii.

Enjoying plants in the genus Aeonium

Aeonium 'Green Tea'
This uniquely patterned variety has brown lines down the center of the leaves and around the edges. It grows by extending vertically and changes color in fall.

Aeonium arboretum
This variety has leaves that extend out at the ends of the stems. The attractive leaves are a glossy blackish-purple. In winter when there is less light, the leaves go green, turning blackish purple in spring.

Aeonium urbicum 'Sunburst'
This variety has attractive leaves in shades of green and cream and extends vertically as it grows. Even a slight graze can damage the leaves, so handling requires care. It is dormant in summer.

Aeonium 'Lemonade'
This variety has attractive light green and yellow leaves. It is something of a slow grower, branching and extending vertically as it grows.

Aeonium undulatum
This unique variety has leaves atop a thick stem and extends vertically as it grows. In spring it has yellow flowers. It is dormant in summer.

Aeonium tabuliforme var.minima
This variety has attractive, dense foliage, and puts out shoots at the side of the plant to form clusters. It is dormant in summer, so restrict watering from the end of the rainy season until the end of August.

Aeonium decorum cv.variegata
Reddish purple colors the edges of the green leaves. In spring the plant has white flowers. It is vulnerable to heat, so care is needed in summer.

🌿 Enjoying plants in the genus Graptopetalum

Graptopetalum 'Bronz'
This variety has fleshy, bronze-colored leaves and blossoms with yellow flowers in spring. It changes color in winter.

Graptopetalum 'Shuurei'
This variety has fleshy leaves in a pale purple shade that grow on the top section of its branches. It is a fast grower, so it is best to take cuttings and buds from it to maintain it at a small size.

Graptopetalum mendozae
The small, fleshy, pink leaves make this an adorable variety. It spreads out in the same way as moss and has white flowers in spring.

Graptopetalum paraguayense
The grayish green leaves are covered with a white powder. It is relatively resilient to heat and cold, and has white flowers with red mottling in spring.

🌿 Enjoying plants in the genus Graptoveria

Graptoveria 'Debbi'
A hybrid variety. It has fleshy, pale purple leaves that extend out as it grows. In spring, it has flowers in a shade of purple similar to that of the leaves.

Graptoveria 'Bainesii'
The fleshy leaves spread outwards as the plant gets bigger. In spring, it has pink flowers. It changes color in fall.

The origins of the Aeonium genus

The Aeonium genus is widely distributed mainly across sub-tropical regions such as the Canary Islands and North Africa. Its name is said to come from the ancient Greek "aionos" (to live eternally, to be immortal). It is these origins that give it the meaning "eternal" in the language of flowers.

Take care not to let water accumulate at the plant's center

Types with leaves that grow in rosette formations in the manner of flowers tend to accumulate water in their centers, so care is needed. Plants are basically structured to readily take in water and store it. This capability is particularly heightened for succulents, which grow in areas with little water. However, wherever humidity levels are high, water tends not to evaporate, and if it is left on the plant it becomes like a lens, which can cause the plant to burn from the sun's rays.

Water has accumulated in the center, causing a dangerous situation where sunlight may burn the leaves.

Getting rid of accumulated water

After rain, check whether water has pooled in the center of the leaves. If it has, get rid of it using methods such as expelling air over it with an air duster or with an empty syringe. If you don't have equipment, you can blow air onto the plant to remove the water. Not allowing water to accumulate allows the plant to retain an attractive appearance. If you are particular about plants' attractiveness, make sure to check them regularly.

Give plenty of water at the side of the plant

When watering, make sure water does not collect in the center of the leaves, but rather water the soil at the side of the plant. This allows for watering without water coming in contact with the leaves. In terms of the amount of water, give enough so that it drains out from the hole in the bottom of the pot.

Don't remove lower leaves even if they shrivel

Rosette-form Crassulaceae put out new shoots from their centers, with the foliage at the outer edges of the plant becoming old growth. For this reason, the lower leaves at the outer edges gradually wither. This may worry many people, as they think the plant is dying, but it is quite natural and no cause for concern. Once they have completely withered and lost moisture, they can be removed from the plant, so leave them until then.

Furthermore, for plants whose leaves are covered with a white powder, take care not to touch them too much. The white powder is secreted to protect the leaves from strong sunlight, so if it is rubbed off through being touched, damage will set in from that point. It's understandable to want to touch these charming plants, but keep contact with the leaves to a minimum.

PART 3

Liliaceae

The tips of the leaves are semi-transparent and beautiful when held up to light

Hints for Liliaceae plantings

Liliaceae is a lovely, low-growing variety with spreading foliage. Its natural habitat includes areas shaded by stones, deserts and so on, and it grows as if it were buried in the soil. Characteristic of the variety is its ability to grow in dark places where little light reaches, thanks to the semi-transparent leaf tips known as "windows" which are very attractive when light shines through them. When creating an arrangement, visualize the plants' natural environment in order to position them in the container.

Create height differences to evoke the plants' natural habitat

Many plants have similar overall coloring or form in the Haworthia genus of the Liliaceae family. For this reason, some effort may be required in terms of positioning of plants and choosing colors to avoid a monotonous end result.

The key when creating an arrangement is to adjust the amount of soil being used in various spots so as to bring out height differences and evoke the appearance of plants growing in their natural environment. When choosing plants, use not only those with vivid green leaves such as Haworthia cymbiformis and Haworthia turgida v. pallidifolia, but add those with unique colors and markings such as Haworthia fasciata, Haworthia cooperi v. pilifera variegata and so on to create variation.

Example combination for a Liliaeceae arrangement

1. Haworthia 'Shizukuishi'
2. Haworthia obtusa
3. Haworthia 'Moe'
4. Haworthia 'Omu'
5. Haworthia cymbiformis
6. Haworthia turgida v. pallidifolia
7. Haworthia cooperi v. pilifera variegata
8. Haworthia cooperi v. leightonii
9. Haworthia fasciata

Remove plants from pots and brush off soil

1

Remove Haworthia cooperi v. pilifera variegata from the plastic pot.

2

3

Once the plant has been taken out of the pot, thoroughly brush off soil. When doing this, remove old roots along with the soil. Follow the same steps for the other plants.

4

Place mesh over the hole in the bottom of the pot and pour soil in. As the Haworthia genus has strong, large roots, make sure to pour in plenty of soil so that the roots take a firm hold. (Here, the pot is filled to about 80%.)

5

Pour plenty of soil in at the center only so as to create height and plant in Haworthia cooperi v. leightonii.

6

Plant it in so that the roots are completely covered.

Position plants close together

Next, plant Haworthia cooperi v. pilifera variegata next to Haworthia cooperi v. leightonii.

Bring the soil up so it is at about the same height as the Haworthia cooperi v. leightonii.

Tips for arranging and combining plants in the Liliaceae family

✓ Plant Haworthia cooperi v. pilifera variegata and Haworthia cooperi v. leightonii up higher than other plants to create different levels in the arrangement.
✓ Consider the colors of the leaves when positioning plants to avoid creating a dull color scheme.

The Haworthia cooperi v. pilifera variegata with roots firmly planted. Planting Haworthia cooperi v. leightonii and Haworthia cooperi v. pilifera variegata in a position higher than the other plants is key to the arrangement.

Plant another Haworthia cooperi v. pilifera variegata. Bring it up close to the first one so that it is at the same height.

Plant Haworthia cymbiformis in the very corner of the container to bring out height.

Next, plant Haworthia 'Omu' at a level about half the height of Haworthia cooperi v. pilifera variegata.

Planting succulents at different height levels evokes the appearance of natural growth.

CLOSE UP

Remove old roots along with old soil

When removing a plant from a pot for repotting or for including in an arrangement, remove any roots that have grown out too long at the same time as removing any old soil on the roots. This allows nutrients to reach the new roots.

Adjust height levels within the arrangement

Position another Haworthia cooperi v. leightonii at a slightly lower level as if buried under soil. Next, create space to make a hole to plant Haworthia obtusa at a low level.

Plant Haworthia obtusa into the space that has been created. Plant it low enough that it is nearly covered with soil.

Next, plant Haworthia fasciata in a low position so it comes up close against Haworthia cooperi v. leightonii.

Use the tweezers to plant in another Haworthia fasciata at the same height as the first.

Tips for arranging and combining plants in the Liliaceae family

✓ In order to create height differences, plant Haworthia obtusa and Haworthia 'Moe' so they are covered in soil.
✓ Add in Haworthia fasciata, which does not have a translucent look, to create contrast in the overall color scheme.

Once the position of the plants has been finalized, press in soil with your finger to firmly cover the roots.

Plant Haworthia 'Moe' in the corner, at a level low enough that it is half covered by the soil.

Plant Haworthia turgida v. pallidifolia next to Haworthia 'Moe', aiming to plant them at a similar level.

Finally, complete the arrangement by planting Haworthia 'Shizukuishi' so it is submerged in soil.

CLOSE UP

Choose a container that evokes the natural habitat

Plants in the Haworthia genus of the Liliaceae family mainly grow naturally in rugged areas shaded by rocks. Therefore, selecting a low container made of stone when attempting to create an arrangement resembling their natural habitat makes for a realistic result.

Illustrated references for Haworthia

Plants in the Haworthia genus of the Liliaceae family grow by extending their leaves out. They grow naturally in places that don't get a lot of light, such as rugged areas shaded by rocks. There are slight differences between varieties, but most are the size that can fit in the palm of one's hand, and their appearance and smallness makes them adorable.

🍃 Enjoying plants in the genus Haworthia

Haworthia obtusa
The chubby, fleshy leaves grow like petals on this cute variety. If it dries out, it will lose its moist look, but take care not to over water.

Haworthia cooperi v. pilifera variegata
Defined by its long, spreading leaves that are a translucent green with mottled markings. Lack of sunlight makes it spindly, so care is needed.

Haworthia cymbiformis
Characterized by slightly flat, large leaves, this plant grows by putting out buds and forming clusters. In spring it has pale pink flowers. It is vulnerable to heat.

Haworthia cooperi v. leightonii
This variety is characterized by blackish purple leaves. Insufficient sunlight makes it spindly, so watch out for this.

Haworthia 'Omu'
The chubby, translucent dark green leaves make this an endearing variety. It can grow indoors in bright shade.

Haworthia turgida v. pallidifolia
A cute hybrid variety with semi-transparent, fleshy leaves that grow in layers. Flower stems form and blossom at the side of the plant stock.

Haworthia 'Shizukuishi'
This enchanting variety has semi-transparent leaf tips and chubby, round leaves. It can grow even in dark places, but requires moderate sunlight.

Haworthia cooperi v. pilifera variegata
Characterized by leaves that are a translucent green covered with white powder, this variety puts out flower stalks from the side of the plant stock. It has white flowers.

Haworthia fasciata
Characterized by deep reddish green leaves with white patches, this variety boldly spreads out as it grows. It does not cope well with direct sunlight.

Haworthia 'Moe'
The semi-translucent leaves are a vibrant green and are slightly fleshy with pointed tips. The leaves may burn in the summer sun, so care is needed.

Remove old roots when repotting

When repotting plants, it's important to remove old roots along with old soil. This is called root pruning. The roots of plants in the Liliaceae family grow particularly large and strong, so prune them thoroughly when repotting.

Pruning the roots when repotting a plant is the key to healthy growth. Here, a Haworthia fasciata has had its roots pruned.

Once the plant has been removed from the pot, brush off the soil and loosen the roots. Use scissors to trim off the old roots.

Prune the old roots so that they are the same length as the short, new roots. Once pruning is complete, wait for the cut ends of the roots to dry out. If plants are planted immediately after the roots are pruned, the excess moisture will cause mold to grow on the roots.

Once the cut ends of the roots have dried, place the plant into the pot for repotting. Hold the plant firmly in place as you pour soil in.

Pour soil in until the roots are completely covered.

Use a stick to push soil into the areas between the roots so no gaps remain.

The movement caused by gently tapping the pot will also shift soil into the gaps. This completes the repotting.

Keep plants in semi-shade, similar to their natural environment

Don't keep plants in a dark spot

As plants in the Haworthia genus grow naturally in a semi-buried manner in areas with plenty of shade, they are able to perform photosynthesis even with little sunlight. More specifically, the plant is structured so that light collects in the semi-translucent "window" sections in the tips of the leaves and chlorophyll is produced inside the leaves. This is why, when cultivating these plants at home, it is best to keep them in semi-shaded conditions resembling their natural habitat. However, if they are placed in a dark spot with no sunlight at all, they will be unable to perform photosynthesis. Conversely, if left under direct sunlight for long periods of time, the leaves will burn, so care is needed.

PART 4
Cacti

Bring together the unique spikes and flower forms

Hints for Cactaceae plantings

When you think of a cactus, you probably imagine an angularly-shaped plant with a hard surface covered in spikes. However, there are actually some that blossom with sweetly shaped and colored flowers or that have uniquely-formed short branches called spine pads to support the spikes.

When creating an arrangement of Cactaceae, it's important to start by visualizing the image or world you want to achieve in the end result. Once this is firmly in mind, consider the color and form of the plants when positioning them.

Choose robust plants that are easy to handle and suit the arrangement

Plants in the Cactaceae family are characterized by the wealth of difference between varieties in terms of coloration, the shape of the spikes, stock size and so on. Start by selecting a large plant such as Myrtillocactus schenkii to be the "symbol tree" (play the lead role) in the arrangement. Next, the key is to choose small plants to set off the symbol tree. Additionally, adding a plant with red splotches such as Gymnocalycium mihanovichii creates an accent in the arrangement. Selecting sturdy plants that are easy to handle and that have similar care needs makes it simpler to look after them once the arrangement is complete.

Example combination for a Cactaceae arrangement

1. Espostoa lanata
2. Mammillaria elongata
3. Myrtillocactus schenkii
4. Gymnocalycium mihanovichii
5. Gymnocalycium buenekeri
6. Opuntia microdasys
7. Cleistocactus strausii
8. Notocactus scopa var. ruberrimus

※ For this planting we are using zeolite, a volcanic-derived ceramic material consisting of silica and alumina. Its composition makes it good for both retention and drainage.

Place mesh and zeolite in the container

1

Prepare the number of plants needed and a container that will suit the look of the arrangement. For a group planting of cacti, a bisque fired pot is recommended, as it breathes well and allows for good root development.

4

Once there are two pieces of mesh in the container, prepare the zeolite. Zeolite prevents the growth of bacteria and prevents root rot.

2

3

Cut the mesh to a size that will allow it to cover the hole in the base of the container and place it over the hole. Using two pieces of mesh will prevent soil from falling out.

5

Hold the mesh to prevent it from slipping while you pour in a small amount of zeolite. Spread the zeolite over the whole container.

Tips for arranging and combining plants in the Cactaceae family

✓ Good air permeability and their root developing properties make bisque fired pots a good choice for group plantings.

Pour potting mix in over the top of the zeolite. Potting mix contains fertilizer-like nutrients.

Hold the mesh down with your finger so it won't slip as you pour the potting mix in. Once the container is half full of potting mix, the plant can be positioned and securely planted.

Put gloves on and start planting from Myrtillocactus schenkii, which plays the lead role in the arrangement.

Add potting mix so that the plant will not fall over. If it doesn't hurt to touch the plant with bare hands, it's fine to remove gloves when working.

Next, plant Mammillaria elongata next to Myrtillocactus schenkii. Position them at the back as if to form a backdrop in the arrangement.

12

Plant Gymnocalycium mihanovichii with its pretty red patches in the center to form the accent in the arrangement.

13

14

Next to Gymnocalycium mihanovichii, plant two Cleistocactus strausii. Using tweezers makes planting small plants easier.

15

Once you've planted Cleistocactus strausii, use Espostoa lanata to fill in the gaps.

16

Plant Notocactus scopa var. ruberrimus opposite Espostoa lanata.

17

Plant Gymnocalycium buenekeri and bunny cactus (Opuntia microdasys) at the front of the pot.

Tips for arranging and combining plants in the Cactaceae family

✓ Make Myrtillocactus schenkii the symbol tree (leading role in the arrangement), and plant in the other succulents after it.
✓ Incorporating a colored plant like Gymnocalycium mihanovichii lends an accent to the arrangement.

Finish off the arrangement with ornamental soil

Once all the plants have been planted, use a long stick to adjust the arrangement.

When you've finished adjusting the plants' positions, use bark to fill in the gaps and decorate the arrangement. Check the overall balance of the arrangement and add more bark to bring out the look of the plants.

Tips for arranging and combining plants in the Cactaceae family

✓ Strew ornamental soil over the potting mix to brighten up the arrangement as a whole.
✓ Plant tall plants at the back and low-growing plants in front of them to create a sense of dimension when the arrangement is viewed from the front.

Prepare ornamental soil (akadama soil) to complete the arrangement. Akadama soil also provides good drainage, but here it is used primarily for its decorative effects.

Spread ornamental soil from the edges all over the arrangement to completely cover the potting mix. This creates a brighter impression for the whole arrangement than if the black potting soil was left bare.

23

24

25

Use tweezers or long chopsticks to slightly move plants when you want to fill in the gaps between them with soil. Make sure not to ruin the plants' positioning when you do this.

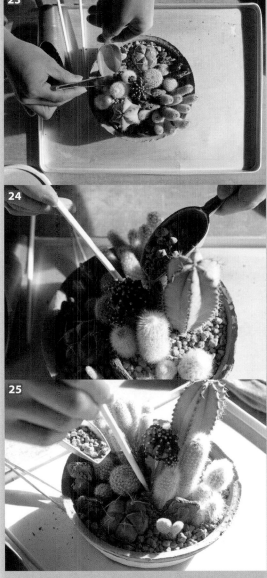

26

Lastly, use a cleaning brush to brush off any soil particles from the plants.

27

The large Myrtillocactus schenkii was used as the lead plant, with tall plants at the back and low-growing plants in the front to create an arrangement with a sense of dimension.

CLOSE UP

Add bark chips to decorate the arrangement

Made from treated pine bark, bark chips make for a stylish finish when added to an arrangement. If there are any gaps between plants, covering them with bark chips will give the planting a sense of dimension.

Illustrated references for Cacti

There is a vast number of species in the Cactaceae family. The spines that characterize them include not only sharp, pointed types, but various shapes such as those resembling starfish and hooks, so it's fun discovering new favorites.

🍃 Enjoying plants in the genus Mammillaria

Mammillaria martinezii
A fast grower within the Mammillaria genus, this plant has a fascinating appearance with its sprouting, clustering pups. It has many small pink flowers that blossom like a flower crown.

Mammillaria herrerae
This attractive variety has dense, white spines. It has a rounded form and puts out pups to form clusters as it grows. It has pink flowers.

Mammillaria marksiana
The vibrant green of the skin and the warty appearance makes this a well appreciated variety. The golden color of the spines and white hairs between bumps are characteristic. It has yellow flowers.

Mammillaria elongata var.echinata
Golden spines grow from the conical-shaped plant stock which forms coral-like clusters as it grows. It has pink flowers.

Mammillaria vetula ssp.gracilis 'Arizona Snowcap'
This cultivar is also known as Snow Cap. Some examples have spines that have been sprayed different colors. It has cream-colored flowers.

Mammillaria bocasana
Hook-shaped spines grow in the gaps between the fluffy hair. Be careful not to touch them with your hands as they sting. The plant has pink and cream-colored flowers.

● Enjoying plants in the genus Astrophytum

Astrophytum myriostigma v.nudum
As it has no spines to protect the plant stock, this plant is vulnerable to the sun's rays in summer. Translucent cream-colored flowers bloom in the plant's center.

Astrophytum myriostigma var.nudum f.variegata
A mutated species of Astrophytum myriostigma v.nudum. As there is no chlorophyll in the mottled sections, the plant is weak in nature.

Astrophytum myriostigma var. tricostatum
The entire plant is covered in delicate white markings. Known as ridges, three protrusions form the triangular shape from which its name is derived.

Astrophytum ornatum
The undulations in the skin are caused by a mutation and are known as bicuspids. Their form differs depending on the individual plant.

Astrophytum asterias
While it has no spines, this plant has round, fluffy spine pads. It has white star patterns on its skin, and the clearer the markings, the higher the price of the plant.

Astrophytum myriostigma 'Onzuka'
An improved breed cultivated by Tsutomu Onzuka, a Japanese horticulturalist. The stars on the skin of the stock have been improved to be whiter, so the stars are white and dense.

Enjoying plants in the genus Gymnocalycium

Gymnocalycium anisitsii f. varieg.
A variegated (mottled) variety. Mutations cause a wealth of variety in the parts without pigment, coloring them red, orange and yellow. Many collectors appreciate the markings.

Gymnocalycium baldianum
Characterized by large, scarlet flowers blooming from deep green stock. The flowers bloom for a long time in spring, forming many buds at this time.

Gymnocalycium denudatum var. argentinensis
A mutation of Gymnocalycium denudatum var.paraguayensis. The chubby, deeply colored ridges have starfish-like spines. The ridges are a deeper color than those of Gymnocalycium denudatum var. paraguayensis and as they are more swollen in shape, this variety is more highly prized.

Gymnocalycium cardenasianum
Attractive, long, golden spines swirl out from the plant's blackish purple skin. The spines grow along with the plant stock.

Gymnocalycium mihanovichii
A horticultural variety of a mutant strain lacking in chlorophyll that is grafted onto another cactus. The red upper section is the body of the Gymnocalycium m hanovichii, not the flower, and the color is the red markings.

Gymnocalycium hybopleurum v. ferosior
An extremely cool variety with strongly structured, colored spines. The spines thicken and strengthen from receiving plenty of sunlight.

🍃 Enjoying plants in the genus Opuntia

Opuntia microdasys
The flat pups extend vertically as they grow.
The rabbit-eared look gives this plant its
common name of Bunny Ear Cactus. The pups
grow in different ways on each individual plant.

Opuntia zebrina f. reticulata
The unique appearance of tortoiseshell
patterns on the skin characterizes this plant.
The tortoiseshell patterns become more
defined if the plant gets plenty of sun.

Opuntia galapageia (white spines)
Originating in the Galapagos islands, this is a
slow-growing plant, increasing by about one
section per year. It has attractively blackish
purple skin with dense, robust white spines.

Opuntia galapageia (gold spines)

This variety inhabits a different island from the white-spined variety. It is thought that it grows tall in order to deter creatures from eating it.

Opuntia rufida

Fine, red spines grow from the spine pads. The plant has an captivating appearance, but it is extremely painful to the touch, so care must be taken when handling.

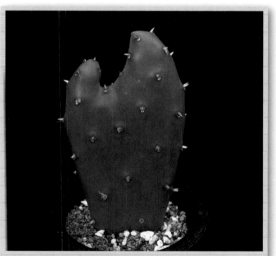

Opuntia ficus-indica

Common names include Indian Fig, Spineless Cactus, Barbary Fig. In Japan it is commonly known as the Ryukaji fan due to the legend that the species was introduced to Ryukaji Temple in Shizuoka Prefecture about 300 years ago and is the oldest cactus in Japan. It is edible.

Enjoying plants in the genus Echinocereus

Echinocereus rigidissimus var. rubrispinus
Purple spines cover the stock, with coloration improving when the plant gets plenty of sunlight. A slow grower, it has large pink flowers. The variety that does not turn purple is called Echinocereus rigidissimus.

Echinocereus luteus
Sparse, fine golden-hued spines grow from stock that is a deep green color. Yellow flowers bloom from the center of the stock, forming blossoms that are larger than the stock itself.

Echinocereus pulchellus
Finely divided ridges give this variety a lovely appearance. The spines spread out like starfish over the skin. The plant has large, pink flowers.

Echinocereus pentalophus
Due to being dormant in winter, the body of the plant turns blackish purple and shrinks, but it revives in the spring and turns green. The large flowers are a deep pink color.

Enjoying plants in the genus Epithelantha

Epithelantha micromeris
Defined by finely coiled spines that blossom with pink flowers, this plant is short and cylindrical in shape. The upper section is flat and soft to the touch.

Epithelantha micromeris var. ungnispina
When it is small, it resembles the Epithelantha micromeris, but when it grows larger it puts out fine, pointy spikes. The parent plant puts out clusters of pups.

Enjoying plants in the family Cactaceae, genus Turbinicarupus

Pelecyphora valdeziana
Delicate, feather-like white spikes cover the entire body of the plant. It has purplish red flowers.

Turbinicarupus alonsoi
Although it is a slow grower, in the genus Turbinicarupus this variety grows to the largest size.

🍃 Enjoying plants in the genus Melocactus

Melocactus matanzanus

This variety grows in a spherical shape. The genus Melocactus can only be grown from seed, and it takes a considerable number of years for a cephalium to develop. It is characterized by long, robust spines.

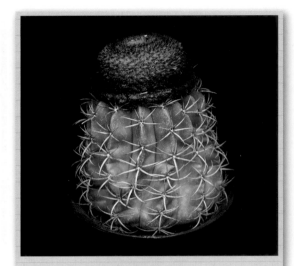

Melocactus species

A hybrid variety. As it approaches flowering age, it develops a splendid cephalium. As it has many flowers every year, it is a variety that is enjoyable to look at.

🍃 Enjoying plants in the family Cactaceae, genus Tephrocactus

Tephrocactus articulatus

The long spines have a soft texture like that of traditional Japanese paper. The spherical body of the plant is gray with silver tones. It is a slow grower and is not widespread, making it a rare variety.

Tephrocactus articulatus var. inermis

A mutation of Tephrocactus articulatus. Although it rarely has spines, they do grow occasionally.

🌱 Enjoying plants in the genus Lophophora

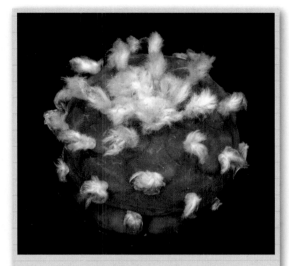

Lophophora diffusa
In comparison with Lophophora williamsii, it is easier to grow to a large size, and puts out pups that form clusters. The amount of hair on the spine pads differs depending on individual plants.

Lophophora williamsii*
A slower grower than Lophophora diffusa, it has a squashed kind of shape. It does not take in water during winter, so reduce the frequency of watering. [Note: Also known as Peyote, this cactus contains mescaline, a hallucinogenic substance, and is illegal in some parts of the world.]

🌱 Enjoying plants in the family Cactaceae, genus Pachycereus

Marginatocereus marginatus
The white of the snow-like spine pads on the ridges forms an attractive contrast with the dark green of the skin of this variety. It is prone to infestations of scale insect, so make sure to keep it in a well-ventilated spot.

Pachycereus pringlei
In its natural habitat, this giant variety can grow to a height of more than 33' (10 m). If it is kept in a warm place even over winter, it will grow well.

🌿 Enjoying plants in the genus Echinocactus

Echinocactus grusonii
The spines of grusonii are short and stylish. A slow grower, it is often seen in botanical gardens and the like, with the larger stock having been grown over several decades.

Echinocactus grandis
The purple cosmetic-like markings stand out on this plant. With plenty of sunlight and exposure to seasonal changes, the coloration becomes more defined.

Origins of the Cactaceae family's genii
The Cactaceae family has many genii, the names of which have fascinating origins. For example, the "Mam" of the genus Mammillaria means "mother" in Latin, and it was given this name because its protruding wart-like spine pads and white resin recall breastmilk. Furthermore, the name of the Astrophytum genus comes from the fact that it has small white markings on its skin which are likened to stars, so that its appearance evokes the image of outer space.

Plants used in the arrangement

※ For Gymnocalycium mihanovichii see p83,
Opuntia microdasys see p84.

Espostoa lanata

A column-shaped cactus covered with long, fluffy
white hairs. The texture of the hairs and the white
color play up the arrangement. Take care when
handling as the spikes are painful if touched.

Mammillaria elongata

The plant stock grows in an undulating fashion,
extending in various directions. With its attractive
golden spikes, sturdiness and clustering properties,
it lends itself to support roles in group plantings.

Myrtillocactus schenkii

Has smooth, attractive green skin. The golden
spikes that grow evenly along its ridges are lovely,
but must be handled with care.

Gymnocalycium buenekeri

A globose cactus with plump, round form and few
spines. It generally has five ridges, but some have
four. Incorporating it into an arrangement makes
for a cute effect.

Cleistocactus strausii

A vertically growing column cactus. The tall,
slender stock is covered in fine, dense spines. It
lends itself to the technique of selecting plants
with different heights and planting them in groups
within arrangements.

Notocactus scopa var. ruberrimus

White spines grow densely on the dark green skin
of this plant, which has translucent yellow flowers.
Even small plant stock will blossom, so it will add
seasonal enjoyment if incorporated into a planting.

Wear work gloves to safely handle cacti

Within the Cactaceae family of plants, there are many varieties with sharp, sturdy spines. When moving cacti into a different pot or working them into an arrangement, they will need to be removed from the pot in which they were purchased. Until you've had some experience with handling them, use work gloves to allow you to handle them safely.

First squeeze or tap the pot to loosen. We will be working with a Parodia warasii here.

Once the soil has been brushed off, insert the tweezers deep into the roots.

Making use of the tweezers stuck into the root section, pull the plant out from the pot.

Grip the roots with the tweezers and gently brush off soil.

If holding spined sections of the plant, put on work gloves. Parodia warasii has relatively soft spikes, but harder spikes hurt if touched, so require careful handling.

Remove any old roots that have gone brown or got fine and shrivelled.

Once soil has been loosened and brushed off, the plant can be potted into a different container or added to an arrangement.

Direct plenty of water onto the soil, not the plant stalk

Astrophytum myriostigma v.nudum

Don't water this way

The key to watering Cactaceae is thoroughly watering the soil. If water is poured onto the plant stock, those with dense spines or spine pads will molder and rot, so care is needed. As a guide, each time you water, give enough so that it runs out of the hole in the base of the pot. In terms of frequency, it's important to keep in mind to give plenty of water when the soil has completely dried out. It will depend on the environment in which the plants are growing, but as a rule, water twice a month in spring and fall and once a month in summer and winter. Additionally, Cactaceae like sunlight, so will grow well if kept in a place that gets good sun and where air can circulate well. However, make sure not to let them get direct sunlight in summer.

PART 5
Asteraceae

Play up unique shapes to bring out originality

Hints for Asteraceae plantings

It's possible to enjoy various types of Asteraceae, such as those whose stems grow upright and those that trail down. Within the plant family, types with round, green pea-like leaves that grow downwards, such as Senecio rowleyanus, are popular. Tweaking the positioning of trailing types within an arrangement creates a look full of originality.

Enjoying changes in trailing plants

Within the Asteraceae family, there are various forms of plants, such as those that trail downwards to grow and those that grow upright. Choosing types that trail downwards such as Senecio rowleyanus, Othonna capensis and Curio radicans is key when putting a planting together. As these plants get even longer after a few years, you will be able to enjoy an ever-changing arrangement. Apart from this, create balance by using upward-growing plants such as Senecio kleiniiformis and adding plants such as Kalanchoe crenata f. variegata to add color for a gorgeous end result.

Example combination for a Asteraceae arrangement

1 Kalanchoe pumila

2 Crassula sarmentosa

3 Kalanchoe crenata f. variegata

4 Senecio kleiniiformis

5 Senecio serpens

6 Othonna capensis

7 Curio radicans

8 Senecio rowleyanus

9 Senecio haworthii

※ This arrangement also includes plants from the Crassulaceae family.

Place rocks in a deep container

1

Prepare a pot with depth in order to accommodate plants that trail downwards as they grow.

2

3

Cut mesh and place it over the hole at the base of the pot.

4

5

Place stones in the base of the pot. Adjust the amount of stones depending on the size of the plants' roots.

Incorporate the trailing form of the plants in the arrangement

6

Pour in plenty of soil (see the "Close up" on p103 for the recommended blend) so as to cover the hole in the base of the pot.

7

Plant Curio radicans. As it is a type that trails downwards, plant it along the wall of the container.

8

Add soil to thoroughly cover the roots.

Tips for arranging and combining plants in the Asteraceae family

✔ For plants that trail down as they grow, position them next to the side of the container.
✔ Plant Senecio haworthii, Kalanchoe crenata f. variegata and Crassula sarmentosa to bring color to the arrangement.

9

Once Curio radicans is planted, create space for the next plant.

10

11

Plant Othonna capensis. As it is a water-loving plant, the key point is to plant it deep within the soil. Once it is planted, use tweezers to adjust its form.

Plant Senecio haworthii in the center of the container.

To add color, plant Kalanchoe crenata f. variegata in between Senecio kleiniiformis.

Plant Senecio kleiniiformis in the center of the container. As this is a large plant, you may need to keep adding more soil until it is securely planted. With its unique, spear-shaped leaves, Senecio kleiniiformis makes the ideal plant for taking the lead role in an arrangement.

Planting Crassula sarmentosa adds white, red and yellow coloration for a gorgeous effect. Add more soil to stabilize the plants that have been positioned so far.

As Senecio rowleyanus is a trailing type, plant it next to the wall of the container.

Together with the soil, push the stock that has been planted already to the side in order to make room for the next plants. Take care when doing this so as not to ruin the positioning.

Add Othonna capensis to bring out a sense of volume next to the wall of the container.

Tips for arranging and combining plants in the Asteraceae family

✔ Add trailing plants in at the side of the container to create a sense of volume.
✔ Check the overall composition and add plants where there are gaps, if you like.

Plant Kalanchoe pumila and add Senecio kleiniiformis. Add in more soil to secure the plants in position.

Use a stick to push soil into the gaps between roots.

Add Othonna capensis around the edges. If you want to cover up any gaps, add in Portulacaria afra Variegata.

Plant Senecio serpens between Senecio kleiniiformis and Senecio rowleyanus.

Lastly, use a brush to brush off any streaks of soil and complete the arrangement.

CLOSE UP

Blend water-retaining soil for use

Plants in the Asteraceae family require a lot of water to grow. For this reason, it's a good idea to use soil with a blend of peat moss, which is a water-retaining soil. In this arrangement, peat moss has been blended with akadama soil, rice husk ash, zeolite and river sand (sand).

There are various types of plants in the Asteraceae family, including vine types and types with hairs covering the leaves and stems. The leaves come in many unique shapes such as round, crescent moon and spear shapes. Astraceae are more water-loving than other succulents, so pay attention to the timing of watering.

Illustrated references for Asteraceae, Aizoaceae, Portulacaceae

Enjoying plants in the genus Senecio

Senecio rowleyanus
Has stems that trail as they grow, forming round, green leaves. White flowers bloom from fall through winter. This plant grows well when kept outdoors.

Senecio kleiniiformis
This plant has unique spear-shaped leaves and grows vertically, blossoming with yellow flowers in summer. It is sensitive to heat, so pay attention to its care over summer.

Senecio 'Peach Necklace'
Defined by its downward-trailing stems which form peach-shaped leaves, this plant has white flowers in spring.

Othonna capensis
The stems trail as this plant grows, forming rounded, purple leaves. It has yellow flowers in spring and fall, and the entire plant turns purple in fall.

Curio radicans

The stems trail downward as the plant grows. In spring, it has white flowers. It is sensitive to heat, so pay attention to its care over summer.

Crassula perfoliata

Has fleshy, whitish leaves that grow in layers and many small, red flowers in summer. It is dormant in winter.

Senecio antandroi

The long, slender leaves grow verticallyon this large variety, which can get more than 1 yard/meter tall. It has white flowers in spring and is sensitive to heat.

Senecio serpens

Has long, slender leaves that grow vertically. In fall it has flowers which look like a mix of green and purple petals. It is heat-sensitive.

Senecio haworthii

The long, slender, fleshy leaves of this plant are an attractive pure white and feel soft and fluffy to the touch. It grows upright and is a water-loving variety.

Family Aizoaceae, genus Smicrostigma

Family Portulacaceae, genus Portulacaria

Smicrostigma viride

The deep green stems branch out as this upward-growing plant gets bigger. It has adorably pointy leaves and is relatively resilient to heat and cold.

Portulacaria afra Variegata

The thin, rounded leaves form layers as the plant grows vertically. In fall, the leaf tips change color. It is sensitive to cold.

Origins of the Asteraceae family's attributes

Within the Asteraceae family, the Senecio genus includes thousands of plant types from all around the world. The name of the genus Senecio is derived from the Latin for "aged" or "elderly person"—*senex*. If you look at the plants in the Senecio genus, you'll see a white or gray pappus that makes them resemble an elderly person, hence the name.

Water plants as soon as the soil dries out

For succulents, watering should be carried out 1–2 weeks after soil dries out, but plants in the Asteraceae family are water-loving, so water them as soon as the soil dries out. They are prone to moldering, so make sure to keep them in a well-ventilated spot. It's also important not to give them too much water.

Othonna capensis grows well when kept outside in a well-ventilated spot. As they love water, it's fine to let them get some rain, but move them under cover during the rainy season when rainfall is heavy.

Check how much the soil has dried out

1

It's important to water when soil has completely dried out. Have a stick at the ready to easily check on the dryness of the soil.

2

Insert the wooden stick a suitable depth into the soil. Take care that you don't poke into the plants when doing this.

3

Removing the stick and checking it, you'll see there's hardly any soil clinging to the stick. This is proof that the soil is dry all the way to the center, so It's fine to water the plant.

4

Check the soil a week after watering and if it is still moist, move the plant to a more well-ventilated spot.

Blend soil so it retains water well

On the right is regular well-draining soil for succulents. On the left is soil that retains water well, made from a mix of peat moss, humus and so on.

When cultivating water-loving Asteraceae, the key is to use a blend of regular soil for cultivating succulents and peat moss, which retains water. Using soil without peat moss mixed into it makes for excessive drainage, meaning that it will quickly dry out completely. On the other hand, too much peat moss leads to moldering soil that causes mildew to form.

It may seem difficult at first, but as you cultivate them, you should be able to find just the right mix for your plants.

PART 6
Crassulaceae

Create a planting that looks natural yet full of color

Hints for Crassulaceae plantings

Plants in the Crassulaceae family differ from the type that form large, individual rosettes, with most having small, thin leaves. For this reason, they can be finely divided to be incorporated into arrangements with many other plant types and are handy as ground cover. Alternatively, if used as the main plant in an arrangement, they create a world in a container that looks just like it has been cut from the natural world.

Evoke the look of a sedum forest in a small container

Create an arrangement to look as if a naturally-growing "sedum forest" has been transported into a container. Prepare a small container to start. Gather together Sedum makinoi 'Aurea', Sedum hakonense and so on for a rich range of greenery, adding unique plants such as Sedum x rubrotinctum and Sedum 'Alice Evans' for a result that is natural but full of color.

Additionally, it's usually important to use dry soil in arrangements, but for the small, fine-leaved plants in the Sedum genus, it's ok if the soil is slightly moist. The fine roots mean the amount of water they accumulate is relatively small, so even if the soil has some moisture in it, the roots will take properly.

Example combination for a Crassulaceae arrangement

1. Sedum hakonense
2. Sedum moranense
3. Sedum 'Green Pet'
4. Sedum 'Golden Makinoi'
5. Sedum pallidum var. bithynicum
6. Sedum lineare f.variegata
7. Sedum Album
8. Sedum makinoi 'Aurea'
9. Sedum x rubrotinctum
10. Sedum 'Alice Evans'
11. Sedum spurium 'Dragon's Blood'
12. Sedum spurium 'Tricolor'
13. Sedum prolifera
14. Sedum burrito
15. Crassula lycopodioides var. pseudolycopodioides
16. Crassula punctulata

Place mesh in the small container

1

It's preferable to use a container with a hole in the base if possible. Many containers for Sedum genus arrangements are on the small side.

2

Cut the mesh and place it at the bottom of the pot so that it covers the hole.

3

4

Remove each seedling from its container. Start by holding the container in both hands and pressing it with your fingers.

5

Hold the root base and gently draw the plant upwards. Pulling it downwards will get soil all over the leaves.

6

Insert both thumbs into the soil to divide the plant stock.

Remove the seedlings from containers and divide stock

Divide stock even further to fit the arrangement.

Some of the roots may have come off while plant stock was being divided, but these sections of plant can be used again, so keep them to one side.
※ See p157 for how to reuse plants

Divide each type into one or two individual plants.

Remove other plants from their pots in the same way.

CLOSE UP

Use tweezers to remove clustered plants
Plants that cluster, such as Sedum prolifera, grow too densely to be removed by hand. Using force to draw them out will pull off the leaves, so instead, press all around the pot with your fingers and then insert tweezers from the side to draw the plants up and out.

Place soil into the cup. As it is a small container, don't use stones, and keep soil to a small amount.

If all the leaves are growing from one stem, it cannot be divided, so prune off the section you want to use. Cut close to the stem when using scissors. The cut-off leaves can be used again.

Hold the Sedum makinoi 'Aurea' at the edge of the pot and pile the soil against it. It's usual to start planting from the outer edges of the arrangement.

Plant Sedum prolifera to cover the other plant. The ground cover has been planted first, so gaps have been filled in.

In the same way, remove the other types of plants from their pots and divide them as required by the arrangement.

Tips for arranging and combining plants in the Crassulaceae family

✓ Plants in the Sedum genus store relatively little water, so it's crucial to leave the roots on when dividing plant stock.
✓ Arrange plants so that they are over the top of the ground cover.

Use scissors and tweezers to adjust form

17 Plant Sedum 'Golden Makinoi' in at the side. It's delicate, so use tweezers to position it into the soil.

18

19 Trim off the overly long sections. Check the overall balance of the composition as you work.

20

21 Position Sedum spurium 'Dragon's Blood' in the center so that it covers other plants, using tweezers to plant it in. Plant it deeply into the soil so it Is the same height as other plants.

22 Add soil if necessary to make adjustments, using a stick to poke the soil in.

Create a bouquet using Sedum 'Green Pet', Sedum pallidum var. b thynicum, Crassula punctulata, Crassula lycopodioides var. pseudolycopodioides and Sedum lineare f.variegata.

Use your hands to gently bring the plants together and hold them with the tweezers.

Plant the bouquet in at the side of Sedum spurium 'Dragon's Blood'.

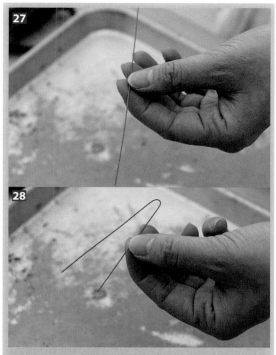

Bend a length of wire in half.

Tips for arranging and combining plants in the Crassulaceae family

✓ Plant tall plants deep in the soil so that their height matches that of other plants.
✓ Bring five plants of different color and form together to create a bouquet.

Prepare wire to secure plants

29

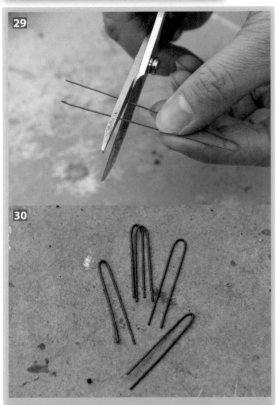

30

Use the scissors to trim off both ends. Create as many of these U-shaped pieces of wire as necessary.

31

Insert the wire so it spans around the stems and poke it into the soil. This allows the plants to be secured as if pinned in place.

32

Add a little more soil if necessary.

33

Poke your finger into the soil to create space.

34

Use tweezers to plant in Sedum spurium 'Tricolor'. As it is an upward growing plant, it's best to plant it in the center.

Tips for arranging and combining plants in the Crassulaceae family

✔ Plants in the Sedum genus look similar, so combine various colors in the arrangement.
✔ Plant upward-growing plants in the center.

35

Intertwine Sedum spurium 'Tricolor' with the bouquet and other plants to create the appearance of natural growth.

37

Use Sedum Album as ground cover and Sedum 'Alice Evans' to fill in the space on the opposite side.

36

Plant Sedum 'Alice Evans' to cover Sedum makinoi 'Aurea'. If necessary, secure with wire.

38

Use tweezers to plant Sedum hakonense in the gaps near Sedum prolifera.

CLOSE UP

Consider how plants will look a year from now when creating the layout

It's important to create a layout with plants facing toward the outer edge, making liberal use of ground cover to fill in gaps. This will result in an attractive arrangement that will envelop the container. Consider not only the look upon completion, but how the planting will look a year on.

Create good balance in a group planting

Use the tweezers to plant Sedum x rubrotinctum in the center of the arrangement.

Plant Sedum makinoi 'Aurea' into the gaps at the edge of the pot.

Tips for arranging and combining plants in the Crassulaceae family
✓ Combine plants in a way that creates contrast.
✓ Use tweezers and a stick to get into small spaces.

Plant Sedum burrito in the remaining space. There isn't much room, so make careful use of tweezers.

Use your fingers to pack plants together while pouring in soil.

CLOSE UP

Adjust soil by poking with a stick

After pouring in soil, using a stick allows for adjustments. Inserting a stick at the edge of the container and moving it enables you to move the soil to the bottom. You can use your other hand to lightly move the plants out of the way to make it easier to work.

Plant Sedum moranense in the area between Sedum burrito and Sedum 'Alice Evans'.

Plant Sedum hakonense in the last space next to Sedum burrito.

Adjust the overall form to complete the arrangement.

Illustrated references for Crassulaceae

There are more than 400 types of plants in the Sedum genus of the Crassulaceae family, with the wealth of variety being one of the appealing aspects of the genus. Characterized by the way they cluster over time, they are tenacious plants that are relatively easy to cultivate.

🍃 Enjoying plants in the genus Sedum

Sedum rubrotinctum 'Aurora'
Defined by its cute, small, fleshy leaves. As it is variegated, it is light on chlorophyll, but plant stock increases well. It has cream-colored flowers.

Sedum clavatum
This plant has thick, round leaves that branch as the plant grows vertically. In spring it has white flowers. In fall the tips of the leaves change color.

Sedum 'Golden Beauty'
Characterized by long, needle-like, bright green leaves, this plant grows to more than 4" (10 cm) high. It is relatively robust against heat and cold.

Sedum hispanicum
Defined by its fine, dense leaves that resemble balls, this plants spreads horizontally like moss as it grows. It has white flowers in summer.

Sedum 'Green Pet'

Has small, long, thin leaves that form dense foliage as the plant grows vertically. The deep green of the leaf color is pretty. In spring, white flowers blossom, and the plant changes color in fall.

Sedum album 'Coral Carpet'

This variety has adorable, small, fleshy leaves. It does not flower, but the leaves turn red when the plant changes color. It is resilient against the cold and can cope with small amounts of snow and frost.

Sedum 'Golden Makinoi'

Also called Golden Japanese Stonecrop. The flat, round, yellow-tinged leaves grow in clusters, forming rosettes. The branches spring outward as they grow.

Sedum versadense

The leaves of this type form rosettes. In spring it has pale pink flowers and it changes color in fall. It grows well in summer.

🍃 Enjoying plants in the genus Sedum

Sedum suaveolens
The rosette form of the leaves characterizes this variety, which has soft, white powder over its foliage. It spreads out as it gets bigger. It is susceptible to extreme humidity in summer.

Sedum oryzifolium
Defined by dense, thin, deep green leaves that spread horizontally like moss. It is relatively resilient in heat and cold. Its country of origin is Japan.

Sedum dasyphyllum
Characterized by round leaves that are a gray-tinged blue. Small white flowers bloom at the start of summer. As it copes well with cold, heat and dryness, it is easy to cultivate.

Sedum spurium 'Dragon's Blood'
The thin, flat, blackish purple leaves characterize this variety, which spreads horizontally as it grows. As it is sensitive to heat, it requires particular attention over summer. It changes color in fall.

Sedum spurium 'Tricolor'

Has attractive green leaves with white edges and pink accents. It spreads out horizontally like moss as it grows. As it is susceptible to heat, it requires particular attention over summer. It changes color in fall.

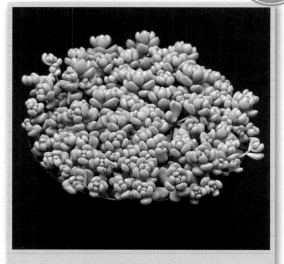

Sedum dasyphyllum var.alternum

This variety has adorable, round, roly-poly leaves that are a blue-green in summer and develop a purple tinge at their tips in fall. As the plant is susceptible to heat, it requires particular attention over summer.

Sedum pallidum var. bithynicum

This variety has slender leaves that are a whitish green. It grows in a vertical direction. It is relatively resilient to cold.

Sedum burrito

The small, round, pale green leaves grow densely. It grows in a vertical direction but the stems trail down. It has pink flowers.

Enjoying plants in the genus Sedum

Sedum prolifera
Characterized by pale purple leaf tips and buds that form clusters at the sides of the plant. It has yellow flowers in spring.

Sedum 'Postym'
Has small, pale green leaves that grow densely. The branches grow in a trailing, upward-leaping fashion. In spring it has white flowers.

Sedum makinoi
The thin, flat leaves spread outwards as the plant grows. Although it copes well with cold, it is susceptible to high temperatures and humidity, so care is needed.

Sedum moranense
Featuring deep green leaves, the branches droop downwards and spring back up as they grow. The entire plant changes color in fall. It is relatively resilient to both heat and cold.

Sedum 'Little Gem'

Has fleshy leaves and puts out buds at the sides, forming clusters. It has yellow flowers in spring and the entire plant changes color in fall.

Sedum 'Little Beauty'

Has fleshy, spreading leaves that branch out as they grow vertically. It has white flowers in spring and the tips of the leaves change color in fall.

Sedum rubens

Has fleshy, densely-growing rounded leaves. From spring to summer the plant grows well, extending vertically. It has yellow flowers in spring. The leaves have a tendency to fall off.

Sedum 'Rotty'

This variety has cute, fleshy, white leaves with a roundness to them. It puts out side shoots and grows in clusters. In spring it has white flowers and the tips of the leaves change color in fall.

Enjoying plants in the genus Sedum

Sedum adolphi 'Golden Glow'
Characterized by the thick leaves which are red at the tips, this plant grows vertically. It has white flowers in spring and the entire plant changes color in fall.

Sedum 'Golden Glow'
A hybrid variety of Sedum adolphi 'Golden Glow', this plant has thick leaves that are a vibrant green. When the plant changes color, the tips of the leaves turn a characteristic red.

Sedum lineare
Defined by its small, fine leaves, this plant spreads out like a carpet as it grows. It copes well with cold but does not like heat.

Sedum 'Alice Evans'
This variety has adorable, fleshy, rounded leaves. In spring it has white, nicely-scented flowers.

Sedum lucidum
Characterized by the red tinge at the ends of its fleshy leaves, this plant grows vertically. It has white flowers in spring and the tips of the leaves change color in fall.

Sedum mexicanum 'Morimura'
The attractive, green leaves spread out horizontally as the plant grows, with the tips changing color in fall. It is relatively resilient to heat and cold.

Sedum treleasei
This small variety has adorable, white, drop-shaped leaves and grows vertically. It is susceptible to heat, so needs particular care over summer.

Sedum x rubrotinctum
This variety has adorable, glossy, rounded leaves. It has yellow flowers in spring and changes color in fall. It is a robust and easy to cultivate.

🍃 Enjoying plants in the genus Sedum

Sedum lineare f.variegata
Characterized by its long, slender, spreading leaves, this plant produces side shoots and grows in clusters. As it is dormant in winter, it requires hardly any watering.

Sedum reflexum 'Chameleon'
A vertically growing plant with thick, narrow leaves. In summer it has white flowers, and the whole plant changes color in fall.

Sedum makinoi 'Aurea'
This plant has dense, delicate foliage and spreads like a carpet as it grows. The whole plant changes color in fall. It is relatively robust against heat and cold.

Sedum morganianum
Has green leaves with a white tinge and grows vertically, then droops downwards. It is sensitive to heat. Watch out for black spot disease caused by excessive humidity in summer.

Sedum makinoi f.variegata
Has characteristic white mottling around the edges of the leaves, with branches that trail downwards before springing back up. It is susceptible to heat. Watch out for black spot disease caused by excessive humidity in summer.

Sedum hakonense
Has spiky, reddish-green leaves like pine needles and grows vertically. It is relatively resistant to heat and cold.

The origins of the Sedum and Crassula genii

The Sedum genus is distributed across nearly the entire world, from Greenland, which lies between the Arctic Ocean and North Atlantic Ocean, through to the African continent. It takes its name from the Latin *sedere* (to sit, to stabilize) due to the way it attaches to rocks and so on. In the same Crassulaceae family, the Crassula genus takes its name from the Latin *crassula*, meaning "thick", due to the thickness of its leaves.

Illustrated references for Crassulaceae (Crassula genus, Sedeveria genus, Pachyphytum genus, Kalanchoe genus, Sempervivum genus)

One of the fascinating aspects of the Crassulaceae family is the variation in shape and form. Plants in the Crassulaceae genus have leaves that layer as they grow, while those in the Pachyphytum genus are defined by their round leaves. Apart from those, there are also many varieties in the Sedeveria, Kalanchoe and Sempervivum genii, so you are sure to find some that suit your taste.

🍃 Enjoying plants in the genus Crassula

Crassula 'David'
Grows in layers of small, round, flat leaves. The backs of the leaves are covered in hairs. The entire plant turns a vibrant red when it changes color.

Crassula punctulata
This variety from Africa has a distinctive reddish stem. It has white flowers and is also known by the name pruinosa.

Crassula arborescens
Has round, fleshy leaves that grow vertically. The edges of the leaves outlined in red are a key feature. It is a slow grower, getting to only about 4" (10 cm) in height even at its tallest.

Crassula mesembrianthoides
Has small, crescent-shaped leaves that grow in clusters. It is a robust plant, covered in white hairs that give it a distinctive feel.

Crassula ovata 'Hobbit'
Has long, narrow, round leaves that are a vibrant green and are delightfully glossy. The tips of the leaves turn red when the plant changes color.

Crassula muscosa
Has extremely small leaves that grow in dense layers on the vertical stems. The stems fall over when they get to a certain height, and the plant has tiny white flowers in spring.

Crassula capitella 'Campfire'
The red-tinged, spatula-shaped leaves turn bright red when the plant changes color. A relatively fast grower, it has small, white flowers in fall.

Crassula capitella 'Trefu'
Has spatula-shaped leaves with pointed tips that spread outwards like flowers. The plant grows in spring and summer and turns an attractive wine red when it changes color.

● Enjoying plants in the genus Crassula

Crassula lycopodioides var. pseudolycopodioides
Small leaves with pointed tips grow densely on the stems, which branch as the plant grows. The depth of its green color changes depending on its environment.

Crassula perforata
Several small triangular leaves spread out to form star shapes. This plant is resilient to dryness and the edges of the leaves turn red when the plant changes color.

Crassula fusca
The flat, spatula-shaped leaves spread out like flowers as they grow. The plant is popular due to its appearance when changing color, as it turns from vivid green to deep red, starting at the tips of the leaves.

Crassula ovata 'Gollum'
Has distinctive long, slender, rod-shaped leaves with a glossy surface. The ends of the leaves are dented and have a slightly reddish tinge. Its unique form gives it the alternative name of "outer space tree."

Crassula cordata
Has flat, spatula-shaped leaves with undulations and mottled dents on the surfaces. The plant extends vertically and branches as it grows.

Crassula sarmentosa
Characterized by the serrated edges of the leaves, which are a pale yellow but turn pink when the plant changes color, at which time the stems turn red. The stems grow vertically.

Crassula rogersii
The spatula-shaped leaves of this plant are thick and plump, with rounded ends. The entire plant is covered in hairs, and it turns from green to red when it changes color.

Crassula rupestris ssp.marnieriana
Tiny, fleshy leaves form layers along the stems, turning red at the ends when the plant changes color. The plant is also called Crassula rupestris.

🍃 Enjoying plants in the genus Sedeveria

Sedum 'Sunrise Mom'
Has long, slender leaves with pointed tips that grow in clusters, with the leaves turning red from the tips when the plant changes color. It is also called Sedum Yellow Moon and Sedum Shintatsuta.

Sedeveria 'Snow Jade'
The rounded leaves grow densely, with the stems growing vertically. It is sensitive to heat. The plant is sometimes known as Sedum Hummelllii.

Sedeveria 'Darley Dale'
Characterized by its long, narrow, spatula-shaped leaves which are pointed at the ends. It is a small variety that clusters as it grows and Is resilient to dryness.

Sedeveria 'Fanfare'

Has dense foliage which opens out like a flower. The leaves are long, slender and pointed, but soft. The bluish color of the plant does not significantly change at any time of the year.

Sedeveria 'Letizia'

The fleshy, glossy leaves turn from green to red and yellow with the change of the seasons. The plant forms branches as it grows vertically.

Sedeveria 'Soft Rime'

Has whitish, round leaves that grow densely in an vertical direction. The tips of the leaves turn slightly red when the plant changes color. The plant loves sunlight and flowers in spring.

🍃 Enjoying plants in the genus Pachyphytum

Pachyphytum compactum v. glaucum
Has fleshy leaves that spread out in a radial fashion and are a deep red color. In contrast to the dark coloring of the leaves, the plant has vivid red flowers in summer.

Pachyphytum compactum
Characterized by adorable swollen, rounded, green leaves which spread as the plant grows. It is dormant in winter, so keep watering to a bare minimum.

Pachyphytum hookeri
Has deep green leaves that are tinged red at the tips. They grow densely in an vertical direction, forming clusters. In spring the plant has red flowers.

Pachyphytum glutinicaule
Characterized by the faintly gray-tinged green leaves with white tips, this plant is a slow, vertical grower. It is also known as Pachyphytum oviferum 'Kyobijin'.

Pachyphytum oviferum 'Tsukibijin'

The rounded, fleshy, red-tinged leaves of this plant are charming. It has vivid red flowers in spring. It does not cope well in environments with high temperatures or humidity.

Pachyphytum longifolium

Has fleshy, patterned, spatula-shaped leaves that spread out in a radial fashion. The plant turns purple when changing color. It is also known as Longifolium.

Pachyphytum cv. Momobijin

Has round, swollen leaves that turn pink when the plant changes color. It is a slow grower and susceptible to heat, making it prone to losing its leaves in summer.

🍃 Enjoying plants in the genus Kalanchoe

Kalanchoe tomentosa 'Golden Girl'

Has long, slender, rounded leaves which are covered in hairs. The tips of the leaves are black, but turn a golden yellow when the plant changes color. It is also known as Golden Rabbit Ear.

Kalanchoe humilis

Distinguished by its uniquely-patterned, round, flat leaves. A slow grower, it does not like environments with low temperatures, and flowers in spring.

Kalanchoe eriophylla

Has long, slender, fleshy leaves with a slightly red tinge. The entire plant is covered in hairs, making it delightful to touch. It puts out stock as it grows, forming clusters.

Kalanchoe crenata f. variegata

Has multiple flat leaves that become attractively edged in red when the plant changes color. It does not like the cold and in order to maintain the beauty of the leaves, care must be taken when temperatures are low.

Kalanchoe tomentosa

Has slightly flat, oblong leaves that are covered with hairs and have serrations at the ends that turn black. As they grow vertically, the stems branch out.

Kalanchoe manginii

Has small, rounded oblong leaves which form layers as they grow vertically. The leaves turn red when the plant changes color. In spring, it has distinctive red lantern-shaped flowers.

Kalanchoe tomentosa f. nigromarginatas

This variety of Kalanchoe tomentosa has fine hairs covering the leaves. The ends of the leaves are a deep black, with the coloration forming distinctive patterns. It is susceptible to cold and is a vertical grower.

Kalanchoe grandiflora 'Fuyumomiji'

Characterized by serrations around the flat, oblong leaves, the vivid red of the plant when it changes color is attractive. It has small yellow flowers in spring.

🍃 Enjoying plants in the genus Kalanchoe

Kalanchoe thyrsiflora
Has big, flat leaves that grow vertically and turn a vibrant red from the tips when the plant changes color. It is also known by names such as Desert Rose.

Kalanchoe pumila
The oblong-shaped leaves have serrated tips and the surfaces are covered in a white powder. In spring it has pink flowers. The two characteristics together have given it the common name Flower Dust Plant.

Kalanchoe daigremontiana 'Fushi You-nisiki'
Characterized by oblong, creased, spatula-shaped leaves with distinctive markings. The leaves spread out horizontally, extending vertically as they grow.

Sempervivum arachnoideum 'Gazelle'
The small leaves spread to form rosettes, with the entire plant covered in fluff creating its distinctive appearance. It is resilient to cold, but susceptible to high temperatures and humidity.

Sempervivum C William
Has green leaves with pointed tips that grow in a radial fashion, forming layers, and change color when the temperature drops. It copes well with cold.

Sempervivum 'Brownie'
Has triangular leaves that spread out in a radial fashion, turning red at the tips and gradually deepening in color. They like sunlight and form clusters as they grow.

Sempervivum calcareum
Characterized by the unique shape of its round leaves, which have pointed tips that turn a blackish color. The leaves grow in layers, getting larger without the rosette shape breaking down.

🍃 Enjoying plants in the genus Sempervivum

Sempervivum 'Unicorn'
Has slender, long leaves that form rosettes. When the plant changes color it turns red starting at the tips of the leaves, with the color becoming more vibrant as the weather gets warmer.

Sempervivum 'Green Ice'
Has small green leaves that grow vertically. It is characterized by the white fluffy covering that extends over the entire plant. It forms stems as it gets larger.

Sempervivum tectorum
Has small, green leaves that spread out in a radial fashion to form rosettes. The leaves are covered in hairs, and when the plant changes color it starts at the tips of the leaves.

Sempervivum 'Tederheid'
Has slightly flat, spatula-shaped leaves that turn a deep red starting at the ends. The leaf tips are pointed and the entire leaf is covered with hairs.

Sempervivum 'Ohbenimakiginu'
Has long, slender, rosette-forming leaves covered with hairs, with the fluffy tips being particularly eye catching. The plant turns a vibrant red as the temperature drops.

Sempervivum 'Lovely Lady'
Has glossy, long, narrow leaves that spread out in a radial fashion. The plant is a deep green in spring and summer, changing to a wine red in fall and winter.

Sempervivum 'Lady of Fire'
Covered in hairs, the leaves of this plant form undulations as they grow larger. The deep red of the leaves when they change color is appealing.

Sempervivum Hep
Has flat, spatula-shaped leaves that form rosettes. The tips turn purple, and fine hairs cover the leaves.

🍃 Enjoying plants in the genus Sempervivum

Sempervivum 'Shanghai Rose'
Has thin, long, slender leaves covered in hairs. The leaf tips are pointed, and the leaves are a vibrant green. When the plant changes color, the leaves change to a deep red, starting at the ends.

Sempervivum calcareum 'Pink Pearl'
Thin and spatula-shaped, the leaves of this plant are covered in hairs. It is resilient to cold, and develops an attractive pink to green gradation when it changes color.

Sempervivum arachnoideum
Characterized by the triangular, spatula-shaped leaves that fan out in a radial fashion and whose surfaces are covered in hairs. It flowers in spring.

Sempervivum jovibarba
Has long, slender spatula-shaped leaves covered in fine hairs, and grows in rosette formations. It turns red when the temperature drops, and is slightly susceptible to heat.

Sense when to water

When cultivating Crassulaceae, keep an eye on when to water them. Check the springiness of the leaves visually or by touching them. If they are becoming shriveled and wrinkly, it's time to water.

In terms of where to keep them, choose somewhere well-ventilated. As they are dense growers, they are prone to moldering during the rainy season, so need particular care at that time. In terms of containers, make sure they provide good drainage and air circulation.

When watering, water in between plants. This prevents water from getting onto the leaves.

If the plant grows too long, cut it with scissors and replant the cut sections

Plants in the Crassulaceae family form clusters and grow long, spreading out further and further. In order to keep them neat, cut off the old shoots with scissors. If these pruned sections are repotted into a new container, they will put out roots and establish themselves. It's best to do this during their growth period. Note that pruning and repotting are not tasks that necessarily must be done, so do them only if you sense the need.

If pruning is not carried out, the plant will grow to different lengths and in different directions. Have scissors at the ready for pruning.

Pruning

Hold the old shoot and bring the scissors up to it.

Cut it close to the stem.

Adjust the form of the plant, making sure to leave the new shoots. Keep the pruned leaves.

Repotting

Once the cut sections have dried out, prepare new containers, soil and tweezers.

Repot the old shoots, using tweezers to insert them firmly into the soil.

The shoots will form new roots. Placing them in a bright spot will promote growth. If repotting is carried out during the plant's growth period, it will take root even faster.

Supervision

TOKIIRO

TOKIIRO (Yoshinobu Kondo) specializes in arrangements made from succulents. Through his diverse activities, including green design, garden design and facilitating workshops, he creates stories (arrangements) that live in spaces (containers).

Inquiries
ATELIER TOKIIRO
ACCESS : 〒279-0042 千葉県浦安市東野2-5-29　2-5-29
Higashino, Urayasu City, Chiba Prefecture
TEL : 047-704-8483
URL : www.tokiiro.com

Message from the authors

"Enjoying the colors of the season" is the biggest attraction when it comes to robust succulents. They change color in winter, bud in spring and once their summer color has faded, they prepare for winter. We create arrangements in spaces that give a sense of the seasons. Based on the concepts of live, let live and grow, we add stories to the communities in our arrangements, which evolve with the passing of time to create miniature gardens. We hope that incorporating DIY elements will allow you to create your own, unique arrangements that bring color into your daily lives.

In Cooperation

Saboten Missile
A shop specializing in arrangements combining cacti and animal figures.

Inquiries
Saboten Missile
ACCESS : 〒299-4301千葉県長生郡一宮町一宮358-2
TEL : 047-536-2339
URL : www.saboten-missile.com

"Books to Span the East and West"

Tuttle Publishing was founded in 1832 in the small New England town of Rutland, Vermont (USA). Our core values remain as strong today as they were then—to publish best-in-class books which bring people together one page at a time. In 1948, we established a publishing office in Japan—and Tuttle is now a leader in publishing English-language books about the arts, languages and cultures of Asia. The world has become a much smaller place today and Asia's economic and cultural influence has grown. Yet the need for meaningful dialogue and information about this diverse region has never been greater. Over the past seven decades, Tuttle has published thousands of books on subjects ranging from martial arts and paper crafts to language learning and literature—and our talented authors, illustrators, designers and photographers have won many prestigious awards. We welcome you to explore the wealth of information available on Asia at www.tuttlepublishing.com.

Published by Tuttle Publishing, an imprint of Periplus Editions (HK) Ltd.

www.tuttlepublishing.com

ARRANGE GA HIROGARU TANIKUSHOKUBUTSU ZUKAN ~ SHURUIBETSU NI WAKARU
SODATEKATA • KAZARIKATA ~ SHINBAN
Copyright© gig, 2016,2019. All rights reserved.
English translation rights arranged with MATES universal contents Co., Ltd. through Japan UNI Agency, Inc., Tokyo
Translated from Japanese by Leeyong Soo

Staff (Original Japanese edition)

Design Masaru Iyama
Photography TOKIIRO
Editing Gig Corporation

ISBN 978-0-8048-5464-1

English Translation ©2022 Periplus Editions (HK) Ltd.

Distributed by:

North America, Latin America & Europe
Tuttle Publishing
364 Innovation Drive
North Clarendon
VT 05759-9436 U.S.A.
Tel: (802) 773-8930
Fax: (802) 773-6993
info@tuttlepublishing.com
www.tuttlepublishing.com

Asia Pacific
Berkeley Books Pte. Ltd.
3 Kallang Sector, #04-01
Singapore 349278
Tel: (65) 6741-2178
Fax: (65) 6741-2179
inquiries@periplus.com.sg
www.tuttlepublishing.com

25 24 23 22   10 9 8 7 6 5 4 3 2 1
Printed in China   2204EP